MAGIC TRICKS

MAGIC TRICKS

Jon Tremaine

p

About the Author

Jon Tremaine has been a world class professional magician for more than 30 years. He is a member of London's Inner Magic Circle, and has been honored by them with a Gold Star, the highest award that a magician can receive. He has appeared on television, and traveled the world entertaining in top night clubs, hotels, and cruise liners. His specialty is close-up magic, the most difficult branch of magic to perform.

Jon has 30 non-fiction books to his credit covering subjects as varied as astrology, origami, balloon modeling, and backgammon, as well as magic.

This is a Parragon Publishing Book

This edition published in 2004

Parragon Publishing
Queen Street House
4 Queen Street
Bath BA1 1HE, UK

Copyright © Parragon 2001

Designed, produced and packaged by
Stonecastle Graphics Limited

Designed by Paul Turner and Sue Pressley
Photography by Roddy Paine
Edited by Philip de Ste. Croix

ISBN 1-40540-409-4

Printed in China

DISCLAIMER:
The tricks in this book are great fun but safety is very important.
• Always keep small items away from babies and young children.
• Children under 8 years of age can choke or suffocate on uninflated or broken balloons. Adult supervision is required. Keep uninflated balloons away from children. Discard broken balloons at once.
• The publisher and their agents cannot accept liability for any loss, damage or injury caused.

Contents

Introduction

Who is the most famous magician in the world? If you had asked me that question a couple of years ago, I would have said David Copperfield. Now, however, the undisputed World Champion Magician is Harry Potter!

I know that David Copperfield is a live professional magician and that Harry Potter is only a figment of J.K. Rowling's vivid imagination, but the fact remains that the exploits of Harry Potter have captured the interest and imagination of children (and adults) the world over. Each year we look forward to his latest exploits and tricks and I, for one, am completely in awe of the beautiful magic that each book contains! I can't think of any character more magical.

As you learn to perform the super tricks in this Magic Box you must say to yourself: "What would the

trick look like if I could *really* perform magic – if I was a *real* wizard?"

Well – we know that it wouldn't look like a simple mathematical puzzle or a rhymed party trick of the type that is so popular with the average children's entertainer, would it? A wizard would just wave his magic wand, cast a magic spell and the "magic" would just happen! He wouldn't need to put something in a special box to make it disappear. He would just aim his magic wand at it and – zap – it would vanish. Do you get the idea?

I can't promise to turn you into a wizard. I will, however, show you how to perform some super tricks

and teach you to present them as if they were **real magic**. Good magicians will fool you but not make you feel foolish. They will not insult your intelligence. They will suspend your beliefs for a while and lead you willingly into their exciting and entertaining world of magical make-believe.

All magicians have to start somewhere. Most start with a Magic Box like this one –

so press on and start practicing. Practice in front of a mirror so that you can see what the trick looks like from the audience's viewpoint. Practice until you can almost do the trick in your sleep. Then (and only then) perform the trick for your friends. There are **five golden rules** that you must always follow:

1. Never tell anyone how you do your tricks. Keep your secrets *secret*!

2. Never repeat a trick to the same person on the same day. If someone knows *what* is going to happen, there is much more chance that they will find out *how* it happens.

3. Practice!

4. Practice!!

5. Practice!!!

SELF-WORKING CARD TRICKS

Time Out

Everybody loves card tricks. Each trick that follows is virtually self-working – requiring the minimum of sleight of hand – and yet they all contain a wonderful "magical punch."

The "methods" are cleverly disguised so that they appear inexplicable.

In this great trick you not only apparently read the mind of your assistant twice but also prove to her that you knew what she was going to think of before she thought of it!

What You Need
A deck of cards.
A sheet of thick A4 paper or card.
A black marker pen.

Preparation
Decide upon a "key" card. Let's say that you choose the Seven of Hearts. On one side of the paper boldly write:

You will
choose the
Seven
of
Hearts!

Your writing must not be noticeable from the other side – that's why we use thick paper (1).

Find the Seven of Hearts and on its back put a pencil dot at the top left and bottom right corners (2). These need only be faint as

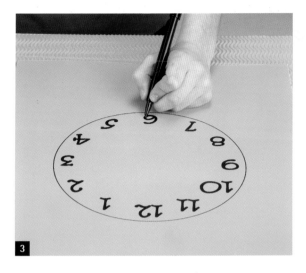

While you turn your back she must then remove the same number of cards *from the top of the deck* as the number she is thinking of (4) and sit on these cards. For example, if she thought of the number 3, she should remove three cards from the top of the deck and sit on them. If she thought of 4, she should remove four cards from the top and sit on them. When she tells you that she has done this, you turn around and pick up the remaining cards.

they are for your eyes only. Place this card in the *thirteenth* position from the top of the deck and you are ready to go.

What You Do

The deck of cards is on the table. Place the sheet of paper on the table, writing side down, without showing the writing. Draw a large circle on the paper and draw in the 12 numbers of a clock face (3).

Ask the spectator to think of any number from one to twelve – not to call it out, just to think of it.

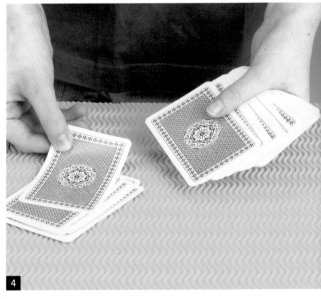

Her jaw drops open in surprise as she tells everyone that you are correct. She removes the eight cards that she is sitting on to prove it.

"OK. Now have a peek at the card that is in the eighth position on the clock (6).

"There are twelve numbers around a clock – right?"

As you say this, you deal 12 cards from the top of the deck onto a separate pile, counting them out loud as you do this. This action reverses their order. Put the rest of the deck aside and pick up the packet of 12 cards. Now, starting at the one o'clock position, deal out a card beside each of the 12 numbers (5). Watch out for your secretly marked card. Remember its position but don't make it obvious.

From your point of view the "tricky bit" is over. Now you must act it up so that it becomes a mind-blowing trick. Say, for example, you have spotted your pencil-dotted card at the eight o'clock position. This is what you would say and do...

"You could have thought of any of the 12 numbers. That's true isn't it? Look at me. Just think of your number...don't say it...just think of it...You are thinking of...the number... eight! Am I right?"

"Don't show it to me – just think of it...You are thinking of...the...Seven of Hearts! Turn over the card and show everyone (7)."

Afterthoughts
This is a self-working trick. The Seven of Hearts will always end up in the position that she thinks of.

Take time to learn the right words so that your instructions to the spectator are crystal clear.

You should get a nice round of applause at this point. Accept it modestly before you put in the final boot!

"Before we started I wrote you a little note. That note is underneath the clock. Would you please turn the clock over and read out aloud what I wrote!"

She reads out your message and your sensational card trick comes to a stunning conclusion (8).

Lazy Aces

The spectator does all the hard work for you while you put your feet
up and just direct the proceedings! She finds the four aces and won't
have a clue how she did it.

What You Need
Just a deck of cards.

Preparation
Secretly place the four aces
on top of the deck (1) and
lay the deck on the table.

What You Do
Tell the spectator that you
are feeling a bit lazy today
and would like her to do a
trick for you. You will tell
her what to do.

First she must divide the
deck into four roughly
equal parts (2). Keep an eye
on her as she does this and
make sure that the quarter
with the aces on top ends
up in position number 4.
If it isn't, casually move it
to that position as you
apparently tidy up the piles
of cards.

Tell her to pick up pile
number 1 and transfer

three cards – one at a time – from the top to the bottom of her packet (3). She must then deal one card onto the top of the other three piles in any order.

You now direct her to put the pile back on the table and pick up pile number 2. Again she should transfer three cards – one at a time – from the top to the bottom of the packet she is holding. Then deal one card on the top of each of the other three piles in any order she wishes before replacing the packet on the table (4).

You get her to repeat the procedure with piles numbers 3 and 4. The action of doing this to pile number 4 results in you getting rid of the three odd cards that were dumped on it and distributing aces to the top of each pile!

The dirty work is done. Now you must "sell" the trick...

"I chose you to do this trick with me because you look as if you would make a good poker player. You have done all the work for me. You cut the deck into four different piles and no one could know where you were going to cut. That's true, isn't it? You did all the dealing yourself and I haven't touched the deck once – have I? Let's see if I chose the right person – turn over the top card on each pile...!"

Watch her face as the four aces appear (5)!

Card Through the Table

In this quick, stylish trick a chosen card is pushed visibly through a solid wooden tabletop. This looks really magical when performed smoothly.

What You Do

Get the spectator to chose any card, remove it from the deck, and place it face upward on the table in front of you (1).

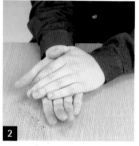

While he is looking for his card (or before if you find it easier), secretly moisten the back of your right hand with saliva, water, or any

other liquid that comes to hand! When the card is in front of you, cover it with the back of your right hand and press down hard with your left hand (2).

Now remove your left hand, turning it palm up to show that it is empty and at the same time fractionally raise your right hand off the tabletop and draw it slightly toward your body. The moisture on the back of your hand will have caused the card to

stick to the back of your hand (3).

Pause for a silent count of three – then plunge your right hand beneath the table (4). Dislodge the card onto your lap (5) and then pick it up and bring the card out again – displaying it triumphantly for all to see (6)!

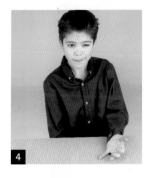

Afterthoughts
To get the full effect from this trick you must "believe it" yourself. If you don't apparently believe that the card has penetrated the table, you can't really expect the spectators to believe it too, can you?

It really did go through the table!

The Impossible Card Trick

This is probably my favorite card trick. I've been performing it for
more years than I care to remember. It is just as powerful now as it
was when I first came upon the principle and developed the trick.

What You Need
A deck of cards and a
dotted key card (see page 8).

Preparation
Place the key card in the
middle of the deck –
exactly the 26th card from
the top.

What You Do
Place the cards face
downward in front of the
spectator at point A (1).

C	B	A

Have him cut off about
two-thirds of the deck
(over half) and place the
cards at point B (2).

He must now cut the pile
of cards at B approximately
in half and place these
cards at C (3). Your key
card will now be
somewhere in pile B.

Instruct the spectator to
pick up pile C and shuffle
the cards as much as he
likes (4). When he is
satisfied he must look at
and remember the card
that he has shuffled to the
top (5) – put it back on the

You must emphasize at this point that you have not touched or even seen a single card and that he has done all the cutting and shuffling himself. Get him to confirm that this statement is true.

top – and then place the whole of this packet of cards on top of pile B (6). His chosen card will now be on top of the combined B-C pile.

Now have him pick up pile A and shuffle them well before placing them on top of the B-C pile (7).

He can now give the cards as many complete single cuts as he wishes over and over again. All the cuts in the world will not alter the fact that his chosen card is now exactly 26 cards away from your key card – so although you don't know *what* it is, you do know *where* it is!

Take the deck from him and spread the cards face down across the table from left to right. Make sure that a small part of every card can be seen (8).

Ask the spectator to hold your right wrist. You say that you are going to attempt to receive "impulses" from him and thus find his chosen card (9). Extend your right index finger and, starting from the left-hand side, begin to move the finger slowly along the line of cards about two inches (5cm) above them.

When you spot the pencil dotted corner (your key card) count this as number

1, and continue to count the cards *silently* to yourself until you have reached the count of 26. Your finger will now be hovering over his chosen card.

Don't pick it up right away. Go a few cards further on – then retrace your steps. Hover over the cards in the vicinity of his card as though you are beginning to receive an "impulse" from the cards. Then drop your finger decisively onto the 26th card and pull it clear of the spread – still face down (10).

Have the spectator name his card out loud and then slowly and dramatically turn the card face up to show that your "impulse" was correct (11).

The "impossible" has been achieved. If it was "possible," we wouldn't bother to do it, would we?

Afterthoughts

If you reach the end of the line (the right-hand end) before you have reached the count of 26, merely continue the count at the left-hand end. His card will always be 26 cards away from your key card.

MONEY MAGIC

Voodoo Vanish

We are all interested in money. Tricks with coins and paper money appeal to people the world over. They are used to handling the stuff and so know what you should or should not be able to do with it. When you start to do the "impossible" with money, people sit up and pay attention – especially if you have borrowed the money from them in the first place!

It is not necessary to be a great "sleight of hand" expert to perform interesting and mystifying tricks. However, if you take the trouble to master this simple "vanish," you will be able to add a special sparkle to your tricks.

What You Need
A coin or any other small solid object.

What You Do
Hold the coin in your left hand as shown (1).

Your other hand travels forward to meet it – the right thumb going under and the right fingers over it (2).

3

Afterthoughts
Well, that's it. Simplicity
itself – but remember to
practice this simple
combination of moves over
and over again until they
become second nature to
you. You must act too –
because if you don't appear
to believe that the coin is
in your right hand, you
cannot very well expect
your audience to believe it,
can you?

Make as if to grab the coin
with your right hand but as
soon as it is hidden from
the view of the spectators
by your right fingers, let
the coin drop secretly into
your left palm (3).

Complete the grabbing
motion with your right
hand – closing it into a fist
– and move the hand away
as if holding the coin (4).

Do not move your left
hand! Merely grip the
hidden coin lightly with
your second and third
fingers. Your right hand is
now slowly and
dramatically opened – the
coin has vanished!

4

The Vanishing Coin

This is "smart" magic! Several natural actions combine to create a
beautiful mystery. Watch yourself perform it in your mirror.
"Mirror, mirror, on the wall.
This is the fairest coin vanish of all!"

What You Need
A coin which may be
borrowed.
A clean handkerchief.
A jacket with an outside
breast pocket.

What You Do
Display the coin held in the
fingertips of your left hand
at chest level and about
two feet (60cm) away from
your body. The back of your
hand should face the
audience (1).

Drape the handkerchief up and over the coin. Keep pulling the handkerchief over your left hand and toward your body (2) until the coin comes into view again. Your right hand comes to rest in line with your outside breast pocket.

Now repeat the above actions but as soon as your two hands come together, secretly grip the coin between your right finger and thumb – stealing it away under cover of the handkerchief (3).

Your right hand continues toward your top pocket as before. As soon as it reaches it, you let the coin drop unseen into the pocket (4).

The handkerchief has now cleared the left hand. The coin has disappeared. Show the audience that both your hands are empty (5) and pass the handkerchief out for examination.

Afterthoughts

This is a masterful piece of subtlety and you should practice the movements in front of a mirror until they all blend into one rhythmic motion. Have fun!

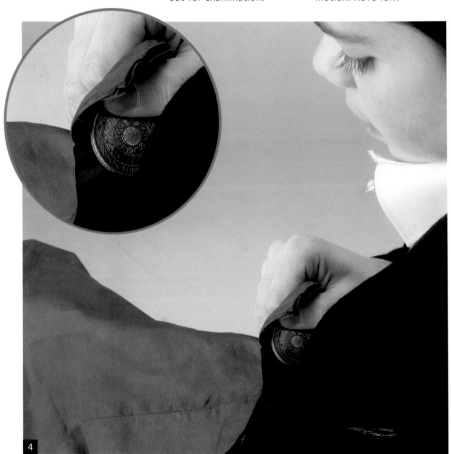

4

The Big "E"

So far we have made a coin vanish in a couple of different ways.
Now let's make a coin appear! You show both hands positively empty
and then proceed to pluck a coin from your elbow.

Preparation
Secretly tuck a large coin
into the back of your shirt
collar before you begin the
trick (1). You should be
seated at a table.

What You Do
Show both sides of your
hands to emphasize that
they are empty (2).

Pluck at your left elbow
with your right fingers as if
you are trying to remove
an imaginary "something"
from your elbow (3). You
have to bend your left arm
in order to do this – which
automatically brings your
left fingers directly over
the coin that is concealed
behind your neck!

Secretly remove the coin
from its hiding place. This
movement is covered by
the action of showing your

4

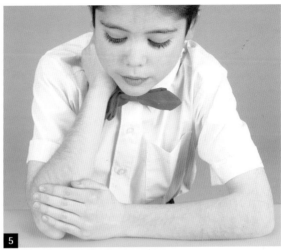

5

right hand to be still empty, having failed to produce anything from your left elbow (4).

Bend your right arm in the same way to expose your right elbow and immediately lower your left hand from your collar with the coin concealed and then "magically" produce it by plucking it from your right elbow (5)!

Display the coin (6). You can now make the coin vanish again by using any one of the methods that I have already described.

6

POCKET TRICKS

The Slave Bangle

As the name implies, the following series of tricks can be easily carried in your pocket and as a result can be performed at the drop of a hat. You will be the life and soul of the party!

This is a very "different" sort of a trick. Its strength lies in its sheer simplicity. Always remember that the method of achieving a trick is not important. Only the final effect on the audience should be considered.

What Happens
A spectator ties your wrists with a piece of string. She hands you a small bangle, having first examined it. You turn your back on her for a split second and when you face her again the bangle is threaded on the string – yet your wrists are still securely tied.

What You Need
Two identical bangles. (The spectators are only ever aware of one bangle!) A three-foot (1m) length of string. You must also wear a jacket.

Preparation
Slip one of the bangles over your right hand and push it up your jacket sleeve until it is out of sight (1). You are now ready to perform.

What You Do
Pass out the visible bangle and the string for minute inspection and then have the spectator tie each end of the string to your wrists leaving plenty of slack

between them (2). Make a big thing of this. It is important that the spectator realizes that you cannot possibly release your wrists.

Pick up the bangle with your right hand (3) – then quickly turn your back on the spectator.

As soon as your back is turned, put the bangle in your inside jacket pocket (4) and, *at the same time*, pull the hidden bangle out of your right sleeve – over your right hand (5) – and leave it hanging suspended from the string between your hands (6).

Turn around – the miracle is done (7).

Afterthoughts

You should be able to complete this series of actions in about three seconds. The faster you do it, the more impressive the trick is.

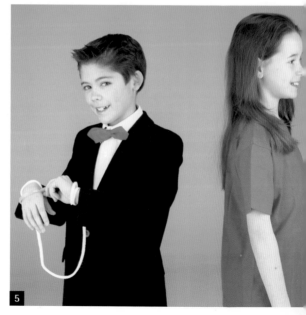

Occasionally someone will ask you to take the bangle off again. You can do this by reversing the process: turn your back and with your left hand pass the bangle along the string – over your right hand – and push it back up your right sleeve. As soon as the bangle has cleared your hand, reach into your inside jacket pocket and remove the other bangle. Turn around and hand the bangle to the spectator!

Color-Changing Balloon

This trick really makes an impact! A very noisy one! The color change is instant and most effective.

What You Need
Two balloons of different colors – say one red and one blue.
A thumbtack.
A small blob of modeling clay.

What You Do
Insert one balloon inside the other (1). Blow up the inner balloon and knot the

end. Blow some air into the outer balloon so that there is air space between the two balloons and tie this one off too (2).

Stick the thumbtack onto your thumb using the modeling clay (3).

When you are ready to perform the trick, hold the balloon(s) by the knotted end. Count to three and then burst the outer balloon with the thumbtack. There will be a loud pop and the balloon will instantly change color (4)!

Penetrating Pencil

Once again everyday objects are used to perform a trick. The props can be borrowed and the effect is very cute. It is a completely impromptu trick – nothing needs setting up beforehand – so you can perform it anywhere.

What You Need
A pencil or pen.
A handkerchief.

What You Do
Close your right hand into a fist and then cover it with the handkerchief (1). Under cover of the handkerchief secretly open up your fist into a "C" shape – as if you were holding a glass.

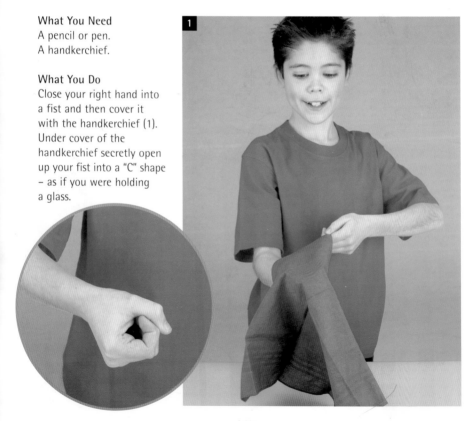

This action will have created a secret tunnel that the folds of the handkerchief now cleverly conceal. Take a pencil and push the blunt end a little way into the hole. Display it in this position as you attract the attention of the spectators (3).

Apparently you now use your left thumb to depress a hole in the handkerchief by pushing material into the well of your right fist. That's what it looks like! What actually happens is that you push your thumb *sideways* into your fist well, dragging some of the handkerchief with it (2). Once the thumb is in, you close up your right fist – then remove your thumb and push it in and out of the well again a couple of times, this time from the top!

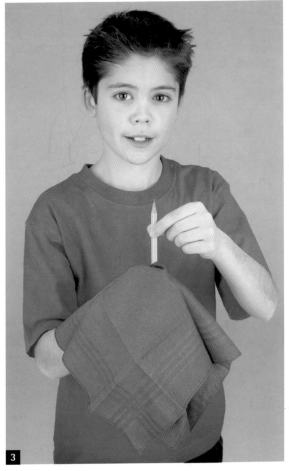

You now unsuccessfully attempt to push the pencil through the handkerchief a couple of times.

"It would probably be easier if I put the pointed end in first!"

Take the pencil out – turn it around – and put it back in the hole, sharpened end first (4).

"Now – watch!"

Relax the grip of your right hand on the pencil and it will sink slowly and mysteriously into your fist.

Delicately reach under the bottom of the handkerchief and pull the pencil free (5). It has apparently passed through the center of the handkerchief (6)!

Turn your right hand over to place the handkerchief on the table and your tunnel will have disappeared.

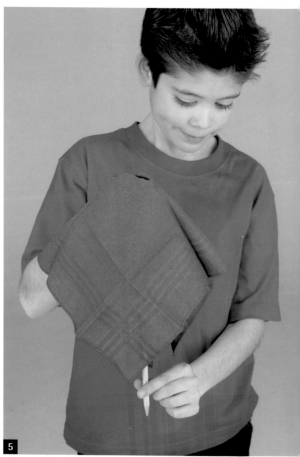

Afterthoughts
This is a very good trick to perform in a restaurant. Instead of using a pencil and a handkerchief, you can do this trick with a napkin and a table knife.

6

CLASSIC MAGIC

The Famous Cups and Balls

Classic magic tricks are those that pass the test of time. They fool people today just as much as they fooled people when they first saw the light of day. The next two tricks can justifiably be called "classics."

When we look through the magical archives, we find that the earliest known magician was called Dedi. He lived 2,500 years ago in Egypt and it is reported that he was extremely fat. He would binge on 500 loaves of bread and a shoulder of beef and drink about 100 pints of beer every day. The Cups and Balls is a version of one of his tricks and is just as good today as it was all those years ago.

What You Need
Three cups.
Four colored balls.

Important
Four balls are used in this trick although the spectators think that you are using only three. *This is our secret* (1).

Preparation
We will call the three cups A, B, and C. Stack the cups together after secretly

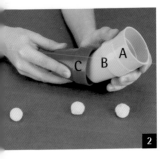

loading a ball in the center cup, B. The other three balls are in cup A.

What You Do
Lift up all three cups together and pour the three balls out onto the table.

Pull off cup C with your right hand (2), turn it over, and place it smartly onto the table – mouth downward (3).

Pull off cup B and place this mouth downward next to cup C (4). Keep the mouth of the cup pointed away from the spectators. If you do it smartly enough, you will be able to do this without the secret ball that it contains being seen. Turn cup A over and place that next to the other two (5).

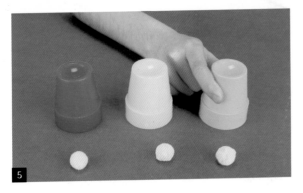

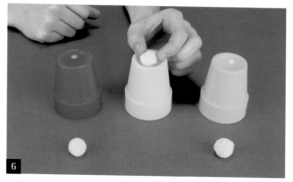

Place a ball in front of each cup. Put the ball that is in front of cup B on top of it (6). Cover it with cups C and A (7). Tap the top (8) and lift up the stack of cups to show that (apparently) the ball that you placed on top of cup B has penetrated the cup and now rests upon the surface of the table (9).

Lay the three cups out again with cup C (which has a ball in it) going over the ball that has just appeared in the middle of the table. There are now two balls under the center cup and one in front of each of the others (10–13).

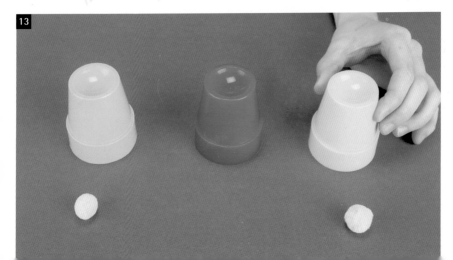

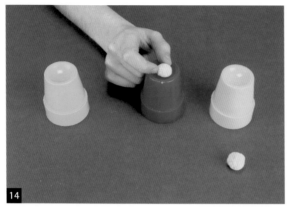

Place one of the visible balls on top of the center cup (14) and cover it with cups B and A (15). Tap the top and lift the cups to show that there are now *two* balls lying beneath the stack (16).

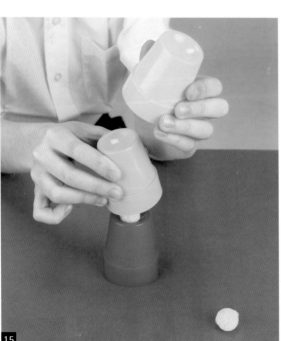

Again reset the cups on the table with the center cup going over the two balls that have apparently penetrated the cup (17).

There are now three balls under the center cup, although the audience will only be aware of two. Place the last visible ball on top of the center cup (18) and assemble your stack all over again (19).

Tap the top and lift up the stack of cups. All three balls have apparently penetrated through the solid cups (20). Amazing!

The Magic Ball and Vase

This Magic Ball and Vase trick was invented over 100 years ago and was first made in boxwood. The surviving vases are now collectors' items. The plastic version that you can find in most magic shops, however, works just as well. The "instructions" that accompany this trick are usually terrible, so it is a pleasure for me to have the opportunity to write some proper instructions so that you may learn and enjoy performing this wonderful trick.

The Apparatus

The Ball and Vase comes in four parts that fit together. It consists of the lid, a half-ball shell which has an extra rim around it that matches the color of the lid and base, a plastic ball, and the base (1).

The basic function of the apparatus is the option that it gives you either to show the vase empty or to show that it contains a ball – even though the ball has been openly removed. To acquaint yourself with this function, first take out the ball and reassemble the other three parts. To show that the vase contains a ball, lift the lid by gripping the pointed top. This shows a ball in the vase. You are actually seeing the top of the half-ball shell. Put the lid back on. This time lift the lid *and* the half-ball shell together by gripping the vase by its sides. The vase is now shown empty.

What You Do

Assemble all four parts together (2). Pick up the vase in your left hand and with your right hand lift off the top *and* the half-ball section to display the real ball (3). Tip the ball out onto the table (4). Put the top and shell back on top

1

44

of the base and set it down on the table.

Pick up the ball and put it in the top pocket of your jacket (5). Say that you will make the ball disappear from your pocket and reappear inside the vase again. Make a few "magic passes" (6) – then reach across and lift off the lid by its pointed tip.

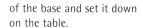

The "ball" is back in the vase (7)! They really see only the shell. Put the lid back on (8).

Say that you will make the ball disappear from the vase and reappear back in your pocket. Make some more magic passes (9)– utter a few magic words – then lift off the top of the

vase by its sides to show that it is empty (10). Reach into your top pocket to remove the ball (11) or, better still, get a spectator to do it for you!

Afterthoughts

While the spectator is removing the ball from your top pocket, you can palm off the shell and secretly drop it into your pocket. If I'm sitting at a table, I will just let the shell drop unseen onto my lap! The vase can now by passed out for minute examination and your "secret" will be intact. In the hands of a sleight-of-hand expert this trick can take on almost miraculous proportions. Please play about with the apparatus. See how you can improve your performance of the trick by doing a Voodoo Vanish of the ball.

Another variation is to have the ball secretly concealed in your left fingers. Pick up the vase with the same hand. With your right hand lift off the lid by its pointed top to show that the ball is inside. Put the top back on. Give the vase a squeeze with your left hand and then let the palmed ball drop onto the table. Lift off the lid (this time by its sides) to show that the vase is now empty. The ball has apparently penetrated through the vase!

47